Markets
Around the World

Casey Null Petersen

Consultant

Timothy Rasinski, Ph.D.
Kent State University

Publishing Credits

Dona Herweck Rice, *Editor-in-Chief*

Robin Erickson, *Production Director*

Lee Aucoin, *Creative Director*

Conni Medina, M.A.Ed., *Editorial Director*

Jamey Acosta, *Editor*

Heidi Kellenberger, *Editor*

Lexa Hoang, *Designer*

Stephanie Reid, *Photo Editor*

Rachelle Cracchiolo, M.S.Ed., *Publisher*

Teacher Created Materials

5301 Oceanus Drive
Huntington Beach, CA 92649-1030
http://www.tcmpub.com

ISBN 978-1-4333-3652-2

Table of Contents

Markets Around the World

Around the world, people go to markets to buy what they need and sell what they make, grow, or catch. These markets are not like the grocery stores or supermarkets you know. But just about everything you can imagine is bought and sold there!

▲ a food vendor at a floating market
in Thailand

People may travel by car or bus
to get to these markets, but they might
also travel on foot, by bike, or even by
camel! The markets are found in city
streets, in deserts, on mountaintops, or
even floating on water.

So, what's on your shopping list?

◄ the outdoor market in Munich, Germany

▲ a floating market in Thailand

China and Thailand are home to two of Asia's most famous markets. Vietnam also has many markets, including a floating one. Spices, spices, and more spices are sold in the markets of India.

A Balinese woman carries goods on her head. ➤

◄ a traditional market in Malaysia

In Bali's largest market, people sell food and crafts.
Women there carry what they buy on their heads!

You will use all of your senses in an Asian market! They are overflowing with herbs and spices that are sold for food and medicine. You will also find golden mustard, cinnamon, sweetly scented yellow **jasmine**, nuts, and seeds. You may also find fish stomachs and "thousand-year-old eggs." Colorful oils are sold from barrels.

These eggs have been soaked ➤ in ashes, lime, tea, and salt

Fresh fish are sold from tanks where they are still swimming. Dried fish are displayed in baskets. Asian cooking uses colorful vegetables that make a dazzling display in the markets.

Asian Produce

Fruits		Vegetables	
carambola		baby bok choy	
dragon fruit		green onions	
mangosteen		lotus root	
rambutan		soybeans	

Europe

Roving (ROH-ving) markets are popular throughout Europe. However, many markets have been in the same locations for centuries.

European markets are known for their fruits and vegetables, cheeses, dried meats and sausages, breads, fish, **wild game**, pastas, tarts, cookies, oils, olives, and truffles.

the cheese market in ➤
Alkmaar, Holland

Around Christmas, there are "Christ-child" markets everywhere in Germany. People from around the world come there to shop for Christmas gifts.

There is a large outdoor market in Munich, Germany, that has been open daily since 1807. People get **truffles** (TRUHF-uhls) at a famous market in Italy. In Paris, France, people **haggle** (HAG-uhl) over prices in the market streets.

Truffles are a type of fungus that grows in the ground.

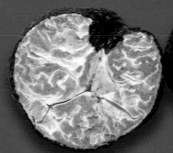

Food around the world may be a little different from what you are used to eating. Which of these would you like to eat?

pulpo de gallega (fried octopus legs) from Spain ⌄

blood sausage from Ireland ➤

⌄ Danish pancakes

marmite (yeast spread) from the United Kingdom ⌄

salted licorice from Sweden ⌄

Latin America

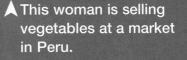
This woman is selling vegetables at a market in Peru.

▲ fresh fish for sale in Mexico

One of Brazil's largest markets is on the water's edge. Shoppers buy fruits, vegetables, and seafood there. Peru's largest market covers a city block! One of the largest outdoor markets in the world is found in Mexico City. Guatemala's largest market sells food, pottery, linens, and **livestock** (LAHYV-stok).

In 1519, the explorer Hernán Cortés (er-NAN kawr-TES) came upon a large market in what is now Mexico City. He wrote with awe about the market, which was arranged like a modern supermarket! There were chickens, pigs, rice, garlic, onions, corn, potatoes, tomatoes, bananas, seafood, peanuts, cashews, beans, coffee, chocolate, **chilies** (CHIL-eez), and colorful cloth.

Mexican markets today

These are the same things you can find in a Mexican market today!

How hot do you like your chilies? In a Latin American market, you'll find a chili to suit every taste.

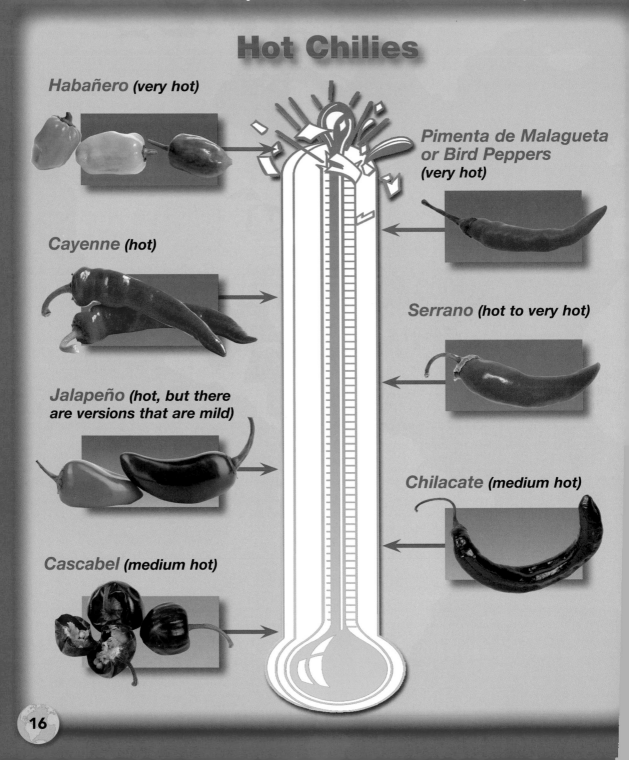

Hot Chilies

Habañero (very hot)

Pimenta de Malagueta or Bird Peppers (very hot)

Cayenne (hot)

Serrano (hot to very hot)

Jalapeño (hot, but there are versions that are mild)

Chilacate (medium hot)

Cascabel (medium hot)

The Middle East

▲ a colorful spice market in Turkey

Middle Eastern markets are filled with many useful herbs and spices and many good things to eat and use. Israel's largest market is in the city of Tel Aviv. The streets of Jerusalem are also lined with sellers during market time. People in Egypt shop at a bustling market in Cairo (KAHY-roh).

▲ a brass and copper merchant in Egypt

◄ a market in Jerusalem

Middle Eastern shoppers can find a world of goods at their markets. They shop for meats, melons, strawberries, brass and copper trays, teapots, rice, beans, **kabobs** (kuh-BOBZ), sesame seeds, yogurt, honey, fish, and more.

kabobs with rice

Middle Eastern Spices

baharat	
cardamom	
fenugreek	
paprika	
saffron	
turmeric	

The Middle East is known for spices. Some spices are made by mixing together many ingredients. How many do you know?

Africa

▲ Tanzania fishmarket auction

At sunrise, people in Tanzania (tan-zuh-NEE-uh) bid on fish at the fish market. Then, off they go to a market across town for fruits and vegetables. At the markets in Kenya (KEN-yuh), shoppers find souvenirs, food, and both new and used clothing. The Casablanca (kas-uh-BLANG-kuh) Fish Market in Morocco (muh-ROK-oh) is a floating market. Fish are purchased right off the boats.

a busy market in Tanzania

a gourd seller in Madagascar

Markets in Africa are colorful. Goods are displayed in baskets on the ground under bright umbrellas. Women wear bold colors and **turbans** (TUR- buhns) that are used to carry their purchases. The air is filled with the strong scent of spices. Africans shop for roots, **tubers** (TOO-bers), yams, snails, rice, spices, herbs, bananas, pineapples, dried beans, sugarcane, live chickens, and fish.

The United States

Outdoor markets are everywhere in the United States. You might find a roadside stand or a farmers market where you can buy locally grown **produce** (PROH-doos) or flowers. Fish markets can be found near the coasts. You might even visit a **flea market** where just about anything under the sun can be found—except fleas!

Pike Place Market in
Seattle, Washington ▼

Washington, DC's Maine ➤
Avenue Fish Market has
been in business since 1794!

▲ a local farmers market

Shoppers enjoy farmers markets because everything is fresh and made or grown locally. At the Union Square Greenmarket in New York City, shoppers can purchase apples, handmade pretzels, goat cheese, and clam chowder. Shoppers in Seattle, Washington, go to Pike Place Market for fish, nuts, fruit, and handmade crafts. In almost every town in the Midwest, local farmers come together one day a week to sell their affordable produce and handicrafts.

On the Map

Can you find the countries that have the markets described in this book? Take a look!

United States

Mexico

Guatemala

Peru

Brazil

Germany

France

China

Vietnam

Malaysia

Israel

Egypt

Thailand

Kenya

Bali

Tanzania

Morocco

25

To Market,
To Market

People buy and sell goods all over the world. The next time you visit a market, think about how many people around the world may be shopping in their markets at the exact same moment, just like you!

◀ Markets around the
▼ world are filled with the
things people need.

Glossary

bok choy—a Chinese cabbage

carambola—a tropical Asian fruit that is yellow and shaped like a star when cut across the middle

chilies—fresh or dried fruits with a strong taste that come in many degrees of heat, used to add flavor to cooking

dragon fruit—a bland tasting fruit with a vibrant outer skin

flea market—a market where people can sell used items, usually outdoors

haggle—to argue over something (usually a price) until reaching an agreement

jasmine—a shrub with very fragrant flowers, often used in perfumes

kabobs—skewers or sticks that hold small pieces of meat and vegetables

livestock—farm animals raised for food

lotus root—the root section of the lotus plant

mangosteen—a red fruit that has a flavor similar to the combination of peaches and pineapples

produce—what comes from farms and gardens, such as vegetables and fruits

rambutan—a small fruit similar to lychee in shape and flavor

roving—traveling or moving from one place to another; wandering

soybeans—a bean that is high in oil and protein

truffles—rare and expensive fungi that grow underground

tubers—the swollen parts of the stem of some plants such as potatoes or yams, grown underground

turbans—long pieces of fabric that people wrap around their heads

wild game—animals that are hunted in nature for food

Index